ANGKOR WAT

Distributed in the British Commonwealth (excluding Canada and the Far East) by Ward Lock & Company Ltd., London and Sydney; in Continental Europe by Boxerbooks, Inc., Zurich; and in the Far East by Japan Publications Trading Co., P.O. Box 5030 Tokyo International, Tokyo. Published by Kodansha International Ltd., 2–12–21 Otowa, Bunkyo-ku, Tokyo 112, Japan, and Kodansha International/U.S.A., Ltd., 599 College Avenue, Palo Alto, California 94306. Copyright ©, *1972, by Kodansha International Ltd. All rights reserved. Printed in Japan.*

LCC 71–158641
ISBN 0–87011–156–6
JBC 0322–783073–2361

First edition, 1972

Contents

Angkor Wat...................................... 7

Notes to the Plates 48

Maps.. 62

Color Plates 67

ANGKOR WAT

In 1861 the ruins of Angkor Wat were discovered by the French naturalist, Henri Mouhaut, who introduced them to the West, where they were soon proclaimed miracles of Oriental art. But Mouhaut did not "discover" Angkor Wat in the strict sense of the word: it had flourished for centuries as a Buddhist sanctuary, and it had been wondered at by other travelers long before Mouhaut.

Over two centuries before, in the year 1632, Kenryo Shimano, a Japanese interpreter from Nagasaki, visited Angkor Wat; and documentary evidence exists that he drew rough sketches of the vast compound, with its many buildings, and that he brought those sketches back with him to Japan. Another early Japanese visitor was a man named Ukon Morimoto, who inscribed a poem on a pillar in a corner of the compound and dated his poem January 30, 1632. There is no question, then, that the Japanese were aware of the existence of Angkor Wat as long ago as the early seventeenth century, as were also a few Spanish missionaries, who visited the ruins around the same time and sent descriptions back to Spain in reports to their foundations.

But it is Henri Mouhaut who has earned the distinction of introducing the ruins to the West and of making the achievements of

ANGKOR WAT 卍

the Khmer empire (eighth to fourteenth centuries A.D.) world famous. In fact, Mouhaut, overwhelmed by the magnificence of Angkor Wat, quite forgot his true profession was that of naturalist and instead plunged into the labyrinthine task of trying to unravel the mystery of the ruins. Sketches and ground plans of the compound that he made in situ he sent back to Europe.

France, which had already established political ties with much of Indochina, made Cambodia a protectorate in 1864, and at the same time initiated a program to preserve the ruins of Angkor Wat. During the following decades other ruins were discovered hidden beneath thick jungle foliage, and scholars of the Ecole Française d'Extrême-Orient spent many years of their lives in an attempt to fathom the riddle of these mysterious buildings. Giant trees that had grown over the ruins were cut down, and parts of hitherto hidden buildings were now visible for the first time to modern eyes; blocks of stone that had toppled down were reerected and restored; and wall inscriptions were translated. For the first time the splendid accomplishments of the Khmers became known to the modern world.

When the study first began, ruins other than those of Angkor Wat still remained buried beneath the lush vegetation of the jungle, and discovering their exact sites posed difficult problems for the investigators. Eventually they made use of aircraft, and once a ruined building had been spotted from the air, much time and money were spent clearing away the jungle and restoring the building. As a result of all this activity, it soon became evident that the Khmers had constructed not only Angkor Wat itself but also numerous other temples in the vicinity, as well as buildings in widely scattered sites throughout Cambodia. Khmer temples have even been found in the eastern part of Thailand, suggesting the tremendous extent of the power wielded by the empire of the Khmers in those early days.

The ruins are unquestionably Indian in origin, but the Khmer temples, with an architectural style of their own, differ considerably from their Indian counterparts. As its name so clearly implies, the Indochinese Peninsula was a crossroads of Indian and Chinese cultures. In the various districts of the peninsula one may see complex patterns woven by the meeting of the two cultures—but nowhere in the peninsula is there anything to equal the grandeur of the ruins that the Khmers left behind.

THE KHMERS

Those extraordinary people who built the great temples of Angkor Wat, as well as those at many other sites in the peninsula, are the ancestors of a large proportion of the people who inhabit present-day Cambodia, although Khmer blood has mingled through intermarriage with neighboring Thais, Vietnamese, and Malays.

Before the Khmers founded their powerful kingdom in what is now Cambodia, another great nation occupied the land. Known to history under its Chinese name of Founan, it was founded by Hindus who had come from India and who established diplomatic relations with the Chinese Han dynasty. Later, other Indian colonists arrived in such numbers that, in the process of establishing their own country, they wholly absorbed Founan.

As a place name, Cambodia appears in ancient times in the Punjab region of northwestern India. According to legend, it was emigrants from this district who first called their new country

ANGKOR WAT 吳哥

Cambodia, but this legend has not been convincingly authenticated.

One theory has it that the Cambodians were an admixture of Negritos (known as Khmer-dom) and Malays, along with many members of tribes of Indo-Aryan extraction. Another theory holds that the Khmers were a Mongolian race (using the term in its broadest meaning), and that a horde of Brahmans from India invaded the country, establishing their own state there after conquering the original inhabitants.

Since the invaders could hardly have brought with them a labor force sufficient to undertake those great projects that required centuries to complete, it has been suggested that the invaders must have made use of prisoners of war to do the manual labor, and have invited skilled technicians from India, which at that time was a highly civilized country. From the architectural point of view this seems unlikely. If a very large number of prisoners of war had worked under the supervision of Indian architects, the result would inevitably have been temples more Indian in style. Instead, the ruins of Angkor Wat, although they manifest certain Indian elements, are not Indian at all in many respects, and the overall style is unique and original. The obvious Khmer elements make it difficult to believe that supervision of the construction of the temples was in the hands of Indians.

What is certain, however, is that the original Khmers came from India, although precisely what route they took in their migration to Cambodia remains a mystery. Two routes have been considered: one through Burma in the north, the other from the south by sea. Geographically, the northern route would seem to have been rather a difficult one, while the southern route was eminently practical, since the waterways had been known for centuries and it would have been relatively easy for a large number of people to have traveled by boat. One objection that has been raised to the southern route was the existence, at that time, of hordes of pirates in the Straits of Malacca; nonetheless, considering the cultural relations that prevailed among Cambodia, Sumatra, and Java, the southern-route theory seems more persuasive.

HISTORY OF THE KHMER KINGDOM

Legend tells us that a Brahmin named Kambu came to Cambodia, married Nagi, the daughter of a king, and begat descendants called Kambujas after the name of their legendary ancestor. The story would seem to suggest that migrants from India proper intermarried with the original inhabitants of the country, but ancient history, as we know it so far, does not verify this hypothesis; it is, in fact, only around the beginning of the second century that the mists that surround early Cambodian history begin to lift.

Chinese chronicles tell us that the country was founded by a man named Kaundinga, who came there by boat from eastern India, and, having married the queen of the land, named it Founan. The similarity between this story and the legend of Kambu gives us some idea of the strong cultural influence of India.

Founan, which lay along the lower reaches of the Mekong River, had as its capital the city of Vyadhapura (which stood not far from present-day Pa Phnom). During the third century, Founan, having subjugated its neighboring states, became a powerful kingdom whose influence spread all the way to the Malay Peninsula. Founan also maintained diplomatic relations with China.

Tchen-la, which lay to the north, along the middle course of the Mekong, had originally been dominated by Founan, but during the sixth century, as Founan declined, it gradually grew in power until the whole country was known to China by the Chinese name of Tchen-la. It was during the middle of this same century that Bhavavarman I of Founan married a Tchen-la princess; then, during the confusion that followed the death of the Founan king Rudravarman (514–545), Tchen-la captured Founan's northern territories, exercising hegemony over the area from Tonle Sap Lake to the Battam Bang district. Having apparently subjugated Saigon to the south, Tchen-la made Bhavapura the capital.

King Mahendravarman, who succeeded to the throne of Tchen-la, continued the war with Founan and eventually conquered its capital, establishing his own capital at Shampupra (near Sambor, on the Mekong). Also near Sambor, Mahendravarman's son, Icanavarman (616–627), who had married a royal princess of the Champa kingdom to the east, built a fortified city that he called Icanapura. Icanavarman also sent emissaries to the Chinese Sui dynasty.

It took Tchen-la about three-quarters of a century to subjugate Founan and to lay the foundations of the Khmer kingdom. On the lower reaches of the Mekong, the land was bordered on the east by Champa, and on the west by Dvaravati. During the eighth century, this Khmer kingdom was divided into two—the Land Tchen-la in the north and the Water Tchen-la in the south. The Land Tchen-la ruled the territory north of Danrek, while the Water Tchen-la, with its capital at Vyadhapura, ruled the land south of Danrek, including the fertile valley of the lower Mekong, all the way down to the sea.

Khmer history still remains obscure, but two facts seem to emerge from the darkness: one is that this north-south division served to weaken the country, and the other is that it began now to be dominated by foreign influences, for example, that of Crivijaya, which was located near Palenbang, on Sumatra, and which controlled the Malay Peninsula.

In the beginning of the ninth century, Jayavarman II (802–854), the true founder of the Khmer kingdom, unified the two Tchen-la's —and Khmer history now becomes less nebulous. According to inscriptions on monuments, he appears to have come from Java— but ninth-century Java was not necessarily the island of Java that we know today. From ancient times onward Java and Sumatra composed the country of Yeh p'o shih; the presumption therefore seems safe that the most powerful districts of the country were the southeastern parts of Sumatra and the western regions of Java. Thus, the Java from which Jayavarman is said to have come might have been Crivijaya. His capital, called Mahendravata, is thought to have been situated at Phnom Kulen (where ruined buildings have been excavated).

The first Khmer king to have initiated the great architectural projects is thought to have been Indravarman IV (877–889); Bakong, which contains the ruins of Roluos, some twelve miles southeast of Angkor Wat, is attributed to him. His son, Yasovarman (889–910), moved the capital from Hariharalaya to the great fortified city of Yasodharapura, northwest of Tonle Sap, Cambodia's great lake, and this marked the zenith of Khmer power. The new capital was known as Angkor Thom ("large town"), although in China it was called the Castle of Yasodharapura, after the name of the king. In the center of his capital, the king constructed a large pedestal, upon which he enshrined a phallic symbol, or linga, and he also built a Buddhist temple there, thus initiating that phenomenal period of

ANGKOR WAT 卍

building that centered around Angkor. Phnom Bakheng, which lies to the southwest of the south gate of Angkor Thom, is thought to have been the site of the pedestal.

Jayavarman IV (928–942) moved his capital from Angkor to Koh Ker, but when his successor, Rajendravarman II (944–968), ascended the throne, he returned to Angkor, which, since it had been abandoned for sixteen years, required extensive repair work. He constructed the Mebon in the center of the East Lake, and he is believed also to have built the Pre Rup temple. The succeeding monarch, Jayavarman V (968–1001), resided at Prah Khan and is thought to have been the builder of Prah Damre.

Then, in the first years of the eleventh century, the Buddhist monarch of the Thai kingdom of Ligore appointed his son, Suryavarman (1002–49), to be king of the Khmers and thus founded a new dynasty, which ruled the regions of the Mekong and the Menam delta. With the new king, who is believed to have come from the Malay Peninsula and to have been under the hegemony of Crivijaya, Buddhism increased enormously in popularity. Suryavarman I erected several sacred Buddhist buildings, and it was during his reign also that the Bayon, the center of Angkor Thom, was built.

During the reigns of his successors, Udayadityavarman II (1049–65) and Harcavarman III (1065–90), the great war was fought between the Khmers and their eastern neighbors, the Champas. The latter, who proved the more powerful of the two, defeated the Khmer forces and sacked Cambhupura (Sambor).

The next Khmer king, Jayavarman VI (1090–1108), became the founder of the Jaya dynasty, which was destined for a long life. It was Jayavarman's nephew and successor, Suryavarman II (1114–63), who built that miracle of Khmer architecture—Angkor Wat.

Other events of the reign of Suryavarman II were a continuation of diplomatic ties with China and an alliance with the former enemies of the Khmers, the Champas, in an invasion of Vietnam. Then Suryavarman made a volte-face, attacked Champa, took its capital, Vijaya, and captured its king.

Bitter warfare between the two countries continued. In the year 1178, during the reign of Jaranidravarman II (1152–81), the king of Champa, Jayaindravarman IV, brought his fleet up the Mekong for an attack on Angkor. Sections of its pillaged buildings were carried back to Champa, where they were used to decorate that country's temples.

Then the next Khmer king, Jayavarman VII (1181–1201), recaptured Vijaya, and took its monarch, Jayaindravarman IV, prisoner. Jayavarman's successor, Indravarman II (1201–43), drove the king of Champa out of the country to Tonkin, and by 1220 Champa had become a Khmer possession. Then the Khmers proceded to capture parts of Thailand and the whole of Laos, creating a Khmer empire more extensive than any before or since.

The decline of this empire began when the Thais attacked from the south around the middle of the fourteenth century. A people who had come south from the Chinese borders, along the Menam and the Mekong rivers, and established their own independent country, with its capital at Ayudhya, the Thais in 1357 laid siege to the Khmer capital and after sixteen months conquered it, taking some ninety thousand prisoners of war. Half a century later, in 1404, another Thai army again defeated the Cambodian forces and captured Angkor, this time taking forty thousand prisoners.

The Thais now raided Cambodia with increasing frequency, and in the course of these incursions the great kingdom, which

ANGKOR WAT 柬

had created so glorious an architectural style, entered upon a rapid decline. In 1453 the Khmers transferred their capital from Angkor to Lovek, on the lower reaches of the Mekong; then from Lovek to Udon; and then finally from Udon to Phnom Penh. It was the abandonment of Angkor that presaged the fall of the Khmer kingdom, which eventually became a French protectorate in the middle of the nineteenth century. After the Second World War, Cambodia regained its independence, but at the present time its future seems precarious in the extreme.

RELIGION

The faith of the first Khmers to come to Cambodia was Brahminism, but they found that the original inhabitants of the country were already adherents of such other religions as Hinayana Buddhism (which had found its way into Cambodia probably around the first or second century), ancestor worship, and the worship of animal totems. Proof of the existence of animal worship is furnished by the *naga* (the stylized, multiple-headed cobra), which appears in legends recounting the founding of the country.

Oriental religions, generally speaking, are not exclusive. The Khmers, therefore, made no attempt to wipe out the various religions and faiths they found established in Cambodia, but rather preferred to incorporate their own religion into already existing ones and so disseminate their own Brahmin faith among the original inhabitants of Cambodia. At the same time, even at the height of Khmer power, *naga* worship continued, as is shown by the appearance of the cobra in numerous architectural sculptures.

Brahminism is based on the Veda, which teaches belief in a universal god; it flourished about four thousand years ago in the Punjab region of northwestern India, around the shores of the Indus River. It flourished also, around the year 1000 B.C., in the country that bordered the upper reaches of the Ganges, but with the rise of Buddhism, Brahminism fell into a decline and found itself forced to revise its concepts. This revision resulted in the creation of the great religion that we now know as Hinduism. Since the fundamental tenets of both Veda and Hinduism are much the same, a number of Khmer buildings are based on Hindu architectural styles.

In order to satisfy the religious desires of the people, Hinduism fused with their original faiths, and out of this fusion came a great number of deities not found in ancient Brahminism. An important tenet is a mystic belief in a trinity that rules the whole vast universe —Brahma, Vishnu, and Shiva. Brahma is the Creator, Vishnu the Protector, and Shiva the Destroyer but also, since death gives life, the Creator.

Legendary heroes were thought of as incarnations of these gods, and this theory of incarnation gradually became so firmly fixed in popular belief that not only human beings, but also animals, were at last thought of as incarnations of the gods. Incarnations of Vishnu and Shiva were considered to be especially numerous, and the Khmers dedicated a large number of temples to these two gods. Shiva was most frequently adored in the symbol of the phallus, called the linga.

The Brahmin trinity has an accepted iconography, as do the lesser gods. Brahma, the Creator of the universe, is usually represented with four faces and two pairs of hands, each hand holding a treasure vase, a string of prayer beads, an alms bowl, and a staff.

ANGKOR WAT 粊

Brahma is often shown mounted on the *hamsa*, the sacred goose, or on the lotus flower that grows from the navel of Vishnu. He is, however, rarely depicted in this fashion in Khmer architecture.

Vishnu, the Protector of the world, was originally conceived as a deification of the power of the sun, and only later was included, with Brahma and Shiva, in the trinity. In the course of time the number of his incarnations grew greater. The cult of Krishna (one of the incarnations of Vishnu) formed the basis of the Vishnu religion of Hinduism. Vishnu is usually depicted as wearing a cylindrical crown on his head and carrying, in his four hands, a shell, a club, an iron band, and a lotus stem. He is usually shown riding on the back of the *garuda* (a mythical bird with beak and claws and human body), although he may also be seen leaning against the *naga* (the serpent). Not all of the various incarnations of Vishnu are to be found in Cambodia; most familiar are Rama and Krishna, the heroes of the epics Ramayana and Mahabharata. There are a tremendous number of temples dedicated to Vishnu in Champa (east of Cambodia), but the greatest of all the Vishnu temples is, of course, Angkor Wat. The portrayal of Vishnu on the corridors of Angkor Wat, churning a sea of milk, is the representation best known to the Khmers.

Shiva, Destroyer and Creator, who is known in China as Maheshvara, inspired the extremely powerful Shiva cult in later Hinduism. His pictorial representation is extremely varied. He may have one face or he may have five faces, but in either case he almost always has a third eye placed in the center of his forehead. Around his neck are coiled snakes and a necklace of skulls; his body is covered with ash; and his hair is twisted into a knot, from which the River Ganges flows. He usually rides the sacred bull (called the *nandin*), and in his

18

six hands holds a trident, a pronged adamantine sceptre, a bow, an axe, a rope, and a drum. He may also be shown dancing and, as he dances, making gestures with his hands to express anger and destruction. Shiva and Vishnu become one in the image of the god Harihara, where Shiva (Hara) is shown on the right and Vishnu (Hari) on the left. Harihara was greatly venerated in ancient Cambodia, and a large number of most remarkable statues of the god have been discovered.

Next in power, after the trinity, is Indra, who was the chief of the gods in the ancient times when the writings of the Veda were most influential. Indra, who lived atop Mount Meru, was the god of air and rain and had the power to create both thunder and lightning. In his desire to protect humanity, he slew demons single-handed and was in return much loved by the people. In his four hands he holds (in the right hands) a pronged adamantine sceptre and an arrow of fire, and (in the left) a shell, an arrow, a fish hook, and an iron rod. He is usually depicted either sitting on a sacred three-headed elephant or riding in a carriage. His image appears infrequently in primitive Cambodian temples. The Shakradevanam Indra of the Buddhists is identical with him.

Other lesser gods of the Hindu religion that might be mentioned here are Skanda, Ganesha, Kuvera, and Kama. Skanda, son of Shiva, is a god of war; he holds in his hands a bolt of lightning, a spear, and a rod; and he is customarily depicted riding on a peacock. He is identical with the Buddhist Shandha. Another son of Shiva is Ganesha, god of wisdom, who has a human body and the head of an elephant; he is usually shown in a seated posture. Known to Buddhists as Nandkeshvara, he was more widely venerated in Champa than in Cambodia. Kuvera, the god of wealth and the master of the *yakshas* (the female demons), is shown with a bowl in his right hand and a bag flung across his left shoulder. His Buddhist name is Vaishravana. The god of love is Kawa, who was depicted as a young man holding a bow made of sugarcane and lotus-bud arrows and riding on a bird resembling a parrot. Kama was also thought of as the god who granted marital happiness. There are, of course, numerous other Hindu gods carved on the corridor walls of Angkor Wat.

At the same time, Buddhism in its Hinayana, or "Lesser Vehicle," form was introduced into Cambodia from Ceylon around the first and second centuries. The fact that no stupas have so far been discovered was probably the result of the poverty of the land at that time, making construction of costly buildings impossible. It is not clear when Mahayana, or "Greater Vehicle," Buddhism was introduced into Cambodia; some say around the fifth or sixth century, while others give the date as late as the seventh. In any case, according to Chinese documents, many people believed in Buddhism, and statues of the Buddha and of monks were said to have been placed in temples side by side. Despite the fact that people believed simultaneously in Buddhism and in Hinduism, the influence of the latter was stronger.

As already mentioned, the people of the Orient do not, as a general rule, insist on the exclusivity of any religion; it was, and is, considered acceptable to believe in two or more religions at the same time. The Khmers were no exception to this rule, for they subscribed to both Buddhism and Hinduism. It seems likely that the two religions at first fought for supremacy, but later combined to contribute to the formation of Khmer culture.

On temple walls we see carvings of both Buddhist figures and

Hindu gods, the figures of the "Greater Vehicle" mythology playing the roles of the Hindu gods and possessing the same attributes. Here the line of demarcation between Buddhism and Hinduism is far from clear, and the temples themselves, as well as the ritual that was employed, appear to have been unified under the protection of Khmer-type gods. "Greater Vehicle" Buddhism, for a time, played an extremely powerful role within the Khmer kingdom because a number of the conquering monarchs were fervent converts, among them Suryavarman I (1002–49) and Jayavarman VII (1181–1201), both of whom constructed great Buddhist temples and both of whom, upon their death, were given Buddhist posthumous names. Nevertheless, the Shiva cult continued to play a major role.

Among the various sects of the "Greater Vehicle," the most widely worshiped were those of Avalokiteshvara and Lokeshvara. The latter deity has thirty known reincarnations, among them the Ishvara, the Maheshvara, and the Brahma. Worship of Lokeshvara was extremely widespread in Cambodia, and gods belonging to this sect are enshrined in the Bayon of Angkor Thom and in the Bateay Shmar.

Buddhism remains popular in Cambodia today, but its contemporary form is of the "Lesser Vehicle" conviction, which was introduced from Ceylon at the beginning of the fifteenth century; the language of the sutras, which was of course originally Sanskrit, has been changed to Pali.

THE ROYAL CASTLE OF ANGKOR

The capital of the Khmer kingdom was changed frequently, but of all the cities the largest extant ruins are those of Angkor,

ANGKOR WAT 卍

in particular the ruins of Angkor Thom. The word *angkor* means "town" and *thom*, "large"; *wat*, which is literally a pagoda, is frequently translated as "temple," so Angkor Wat may be thought of as the Temple of the Royal Castle.

Yasovarman (889–910), the founder of Angkor, built the royal city of Yasodharapura (northwest of the great lake now known as Tonle Sap), and in the center of the city he erected a pedestal upon which he enshrined the linga, the phallus that was one of the forms of Shiva. Yasovarman thus set the stage for the tremendous architectural drama that was to be enacted in and around Angkor.

The central pedestal itself, however, was not reliably identified until research determined that it was identical with the Phnom Bakheng situated near the south gate of the present-day ruins of Angkor Thom. As a result of aerial reconnaissance and excavations, the ruins of a great castle were discovered, part of which overlapped Angkor Thom. The presumption was made that the castle, with Phnom Bakheng in its center, was constructed by Yasovarman. It was more than double the size of Angkor Thom, and it faced in the same direction.

It is conjectured that this site was chosen for the castle because it possessed a convenient hill upon which the central pedestal might be erected and also because the Siem Reap River flowed along its eastern border. Using the available water, Yasovarman undertook the arduous construction of two great reservoirs at Yasodharapura, to the east and west of the castle. Ruins reveal that the rectangular east reservoir measured 2,056 yards from north to south and 7,650 yards from east to west; the west reservoir, which was much larger, measured 2,515 yards from north to south and 8,749 yards from east to west. The water was employed largely for purposes of irrigation. The walls of both reservoirs were quite high, and the bottom of the west lake had not been dug out. The city castle of Yasodharapura was the Khmer capital for only about twenty years, and in the year 921, it was transferred to Koh Ker, about sixty miles northeast of Angkor. Thus, the district of Angkor came to be forgotten for a while.

According to available records, the capital was once again returned to Angkor when Rajendravarman II (944–968) ascended the throne. The site of this new capital was apparently not, however, identical with that of Yasovarman's capital, since Rajendravarman left the Phnom Bakheng (which would have been indispensible to the construction of a city) unfinished. In the center of the city, at the point where the axis of the Phnom Bakheng crossed that of the east reservoir, the king constructed the pyramid of Phimeanakas. Only its foundation remains today, indicating that the building itself was probably wood. Angkor flourished during this reign, and such temples as East Mebon, Pre Rup, and Prasat Bat Chum were built in the neighborhood of Angkor Thom. The walls of the city are no longer standing, but since the Phimeanakas pyramid is situated equidistant from the south and east walls of Angkor Thom, the east bank of the west reservoir, and the north bank of the reservoir behind Prah Khan, the fortified city that stood there probably used these places for its outer walls.

During the reign of Jayavarman V (Rajendravarman's successor), the outer tence of the Phimeanakas and the royal palace was apparently replaced by a thick laterite wall. Apparently also, the Ta Keo outside the east gate and the North Klean facing the main square were built during the same reign.

After Udayadityavarman II came to the throne in 1049, the city center appears to have been moved from the Phimeanakas to the Baphuon in the south. The only construction of this particular period known today is the tower of the West Mebon (at the west reservoir). The entire area of this new capital is not easily deciphered, but it appears to resemble somewhat ancient Japan's imperial capital of Heijokyo (710–84). There the place where the emperor carried out his duties as a sovereign (the Chodoin), near the main hall, was not the original building, but was constructed somewhat to the east of the original; hence, it was not situated on the central line of Heijokyo. The Phimeanakas and the Baphuon appear to bear the same relationship as the Chodoin did to Heijokyo.

Jayavarman VII (1181–1220) succeeded to the throne just after the invasion by the Champa fleet, which destroyed the capital and looted it of many of its treasures. Presumably most of the buildings of this period were of wood. With the departure of the Champa conquerors, the new king sought to invigorate the declining Khmer empire and bent every effort toward the construction of a new capital with its center southeast of Baphuon. In order to reduce expenses of construction, the king lessened the area of the new capital. That new city is what we now know as Angkor Thom.

Jayavarman VII first erected a Bayon in the center of the capital; he then built a series of outer walls around the city itself but did not build walls around the Bayon. (It was discovered recently that this Bayon was a Jayavarman VII construction and not, as originally thought, Yasovarman's central pedestal.) The new king also laid down four wide roads but, because of Phnom Bakheng, continued to use the old north-south road as a main artery. Of the new roads, one led to the Gate of the Dead (on the east) while another led to the west gate. The fifth gate was known as the Gate of

Victory. The royal palace itself stood to the northwest of the Bayon.

The Bayon (aside from the five gates and the castle walls) was Jayavarman's only construction within Angkor Thom; most of its other remains are older than the Bayon. Since the area within the walls of Angkor Thom was too small to permit the construction of a large number of temples, sites were sought outside the city walls, such as Prah Khan (near the northeast corner of Thom), Neak Pean (to the east of Prah Khan), and Ta Prohm and Banteay Kedei (to the east of Thom). The large scale of all of these buildings gives some indication of the wealth and power of the king.

Then, around the year 1431, Angkor Thom fell into desuetude and ceased to be the capital of the kingdom.

GROUND PLANS OF KHMER TEMPLES

The architectural style of Khmer memorial structures is for all practical purposes identical, no matter whether the buildings were intended for Buddhist or Hindu worship; the only distinction lies in the nature of the wall carvings. Ground plans of the buildings, however, are extremely diversified.

Khmer temples, with their origins in the *sikharas* (temple tower) architecture of India, are always tower shaped, but their outward appearance, despite their Indian affiliations, is unique. The Khmers' towered temples are customarily surrounded by corridors and walls, and the ground plan of the temple depends directly on the number of its towers and consequently upon the number of corridors and walls surrounding the towers. Exteriors differ greatly also in appearance depending upon whether or not the temples are of pyramidal form.

ANGKOR WAT 宝

The simplest style (of which there are numerous examples) consists of one independent tower. Most extant examples of this single-tower type date from the seventh century, when Khmer architecture was just beginning to develop its individual characteristics. Eminently representative of this type is the Bakong in the Roluos group, which consists of a huge tower standing in the center of a pyramidal foundation. The Baphuon, in Angkor Thom, although an independent tower also, is slightly different from the Bakong in that it is surrounded by three tiers of pyramidal corridors, in this respect approaching the type of architecture predominant at Angkor Wat. The temples Nos. 1–3 of the Prah Palilay and the Prah Pithu groups also have independent towers, suggesting that the wood buildings of Phimeanakas and the West Mebon also stood independently.

In more than a few instances a room was constructed in front of the tower for the offering of prayers: a classic example of this is to be found in the Banteay Samre, a magnificent building encircled by corridors. Of the same architectural style are the Chau Say Tevoda and the Thommanon, both situated near the Gate of Victory at Angkor Thom and both surrounded by walls. The former building has not been restored, but the latter has recently undergone extensive restoration and may now be seen almost as it was originally conceived. Prah Khan, north of Angkor Thom, possesses a number of small towers placed irregularly in its corridors, but its central section may be considered of the same type.

The next most frequent form is that in which five towers are arranged like the five dots of a pair of dice. Examples of this architectural style are Pre Rup, East Mebon, and Ta Keo, all of which have pyramidal foundations rising to a platform upon which the five towers have been constructed.

The origin of this five-towered architectural style is thought to be the great tower of Budh Gaya in India, which is presently used as a Hindu temple but which was originally a Buddhist temple. It is an architectural form found in many parts of Asia: Wat Chet Yot near Chiengmai, in Thailand, is patterned after this style, and an even more famous example may be found in the Diamond Temple within the Ta-Cheng-Chiao-ssu temple compound in Peking. Java and Burma also possess buildings in the five-tower style, while Japan has a type of tower (called *yugi*) on the roof of which were erected multiple towers, each surrounded by five bands.

This same style also influenced Indian Islamic architecture, the most famous example being the Taj Mahal, which has a great dome in the center and a smaller dome in each of the four corners, giving an impression of five towers soaring up into the sky. This same type of architectural style is to be found in a number of other Islamic buildings in India: it has been suggested, interestingly enough, that the five towers represent the five treasures of Buddhism and must derive from Indian thought, since nowhere else in the world is Islamic architecture characterized by the five-tower style. Other scholars suggest that the five towers symbolize the form of Mount Meru (the sacred mountain in the middle of the earth, which is the home of the gods). In either case, it seems likely that the five-tower style of Khmer architecture was imported from India and had its origin in Buddhist theology.

Angkor Wat is a variation of this five-towered style; if the four corner towers are joined by corridors, the result is the Angkor Wat style of architecture composed of three-tiered corridors of pyramidal form and precise geometric pattern. At Beng Mealea, the pyramidal foundation has disappeared, and the ground plan is similar to that

ANGKOR WAT 圖

of Angkor Wat. Of the same type are the temples of Banteay Kedei and of Ta Prohm.

In addition to the one-tower and five-tower styles of architecture, there are several existing temples characterized by three towers and by six towers. Examples of the former are Phnom Krom and Banteay Srei, in which the three towers are arranged in a straight line with the central tower the tallest of the three. Banteay Srei has an outer prayer room in front of the central tower, and Phnom Krom is situated on the summit of a high hill. Neither building has a pyramidal foundation.

In the six-tower style, two rows of three towers each are arranged in parallel lines. Representative of this type is Prah Ko, where the central tower in the first row is slightly higher than the two on either side of it. Lolei was also conceived in the six-tower style and (like both the East and West Mebon) was built on a small island in the center of an artificial lake; however, only four of Lolei's towers, which are arranged on a common foundation, were finally constructed.

In studying the development of these diverse architectural styles, one concludes that the one-tower style was the most ancient of all. Examples stretch from Sambor (seventh century) through the highly representative Bakong (end of the ninth century) all the way up to the Baphuon (middle of the eleventh century), suggesting the long life that this particular style enjoyed in the history and development of Khmer architecture. All three of these one-tower buildings have pyramidal foundations.

India also possesses numerous examples of temples in which outer prayer halls have been built in front of towers. With Hindu temples, the main buildings stand in a straight line, and the principal building (*sikharas*) is situated at the farthest end, with the prayer hall (*jagamohan*) in front of it. There are also instances in which a dancing hall (*nat mandir*) was placed in front of the *jagamohan*, and a sacrificial hall (*bhog mandir*) in front of the *nat mandir*. Khmer architecture has no example of a single building that possesses all four halls; Banteay Samre is illustrative of a temple with an outer prayer hall.

To fulfill its function, the dancing hall must have been an extremely spacious construction, such as the Jagannath of Puri, in India, a tremendous tenth-century hall with a large number of pillars. Although this particular type of dancing hall is not to be found in Khmer architecture, there do exist examples of dancing halls with pillared corridors in the shape of the Chinese character *ta*: 田. In twelfth-century Buddhist temples, such as Prah Khan, Banteay Kedei, and Ta Prohm, these halls are located on the east side in front of the second corridor. This same type of dancing hall was constructed even earlier, as at Angkor Wat and Beng Mealea, but here the halls were introduced between the second and third corridors to create a form shaped like a capital H with an additional vertical stroke in the center. There can be no doubt that these were intended to be dancing halls, since the figures of *apsaras* (heavenly dancers) are to be seen almost everywhere on the walls.

Both the Angkor Wat and Beng Mealea are products of the beginning of the twelfth century. There are no earlier ruins indicating that the dancing hall was in existence. In the ruins of Prah Khan, an oratory had been attached in front of the tower. The same can be said in the case of Beng Mealea, but the central part is not symmetrical on four sides. However, in the case of Angkor Wat, the central part shows this symmetry on four sides. In other words, part of the corridor leading from the central tower to the four central entrances

ANGKOR WAT 🔆

of the third corridor had been expanded to the right and left, forming, presumably, the oratory.

It would seem that the pyramidal foundation, such as is found in the Bakong in the Roluos group and in the Phnom Bakheng, was first used by Khmer architects around the end of the ninth century. During the following century it grew in popularity, as is evidenced by the fact that the East Mebon, Pre Rup, and Ta Keo all make use of the pyramidal foundation.

Angkor Wat is characterized by the five-tower style of architecture as well as by corridors; these are Hindu elements, but they have been arranged in the most precise geometrical form. Thus, although the ground plan is extremely complex, the arrangement of the buildings finds no parallel in India, suggesting the high creative ability of native Khmer architects. It is astonishing that, using such an intricate ground plan, they were still able to create a three-dimensional effect of such grandeur.

Some critics claim that artistically Angkor Wat cannot be compared with the Borobudur of Java, and indeed from the point of view of the details of architectural sculpture, Angkor Wat is inferior to Borobudur. But this is largely a question of chronology and does not indicate that the Khmers were lacking in artistic ability. The carvings they produced before the ninth century are magnificent, and those of Banteay Srei, which were done in the middle of the tenth century, are extremely fine. If we find the sculptures of Angkor Wat, which were done later, somewhat inferior, we should recollect that the true greatness of Angkor Wat lies in its architecture rather than in its sculpture.

These carvings are to be found on the inner walls of the first corridor, which is of dual structure. The circumference of the cor-

ridor is 2,625 feet; it is divided into eight sections by its eight entrances, four of which are at the corners and four in between. On
the walls, which have a total area of 2,190 square yards, are sculptured episodes from the Mahabharata and the Ramayana; the fact that
the carvings may be viewed from outside the first corridor suggests
that their purpose may have been the enlightenment of the common
people. Wall carvings in the Bayon between the first and second
corridors are concerned with the achievements of the Khmer kings
and may well have served the same purpose as those of Angkor
Wat.

Khmer temples almost invariably faced toward the east, and the
eastern facade possessed a tower-gate that served as the main entrance. Angkor Wat, an exception to this rule, faces west. Because
of this, some scholars hypothesized that Angkor Wat was a funerary
or mortuary temple, a royal mausoleum in fact, dedicated to the god
Vishnu into whom King Suryavarman II, builder of the temple,
was to be absorbed upon his death. Stone coffins have been excavated from under the central point of several Khmer temples, suggesting that the temples were in fact funerary, but no such stone
coffin has been found at Angkor Wat. There are indications that
burials were made some ninety feet under the central point of the
temple, but these were probably Buddhist reburials. All temples of
the Angkor period were dedicated either to the gods or to the Buddha and were, at the same time, royal mausoleums. Therefore, it
would be inaccurate to say that Angkor Wat alone was a funerary
temple. It faced west for a very simple reason: it was situated on
the east side of the road leading to Angkor Thom.

31

ANGKOR WAT 图

The question of how the many buildings erected in the vicinity of Angkor Wat were constructed poses some interesting problems. However great the power of the Khmer kings may have been, it is truly astonishing that, at a time when methods of transportation were so primitive, the Khmers were able to amass such mountains of building materials and to create such magnificent edifices demonstrating so high a degree of technological skill.

Two kinds of material used in the construction of Angkor Wat have endured: laterite and sandstone. The wood out of which roofs were made has rotted away and wholly disappeared.

Laterite is not a stone but rather a sort of subsoil found not only in Cambodia but also in Thailand, India, and other equatorial regions. It first became known to the West in the early part of the nineteenth century, when a Scot, traveling through south India, came across it. It cannot be finely carved, and so is used only in such rough work as walls and roofs; then, over the laterite framework, blocks of sandstone are installed for the sculptor to work on.

When still underground, laterite, because of its high water content, is comparatively soft, but once it is exposed to sunlight it becomes so hard that it is extremely difficult to carve. When it is to be quarried, some twelve inches of surface soil are first removed, then the exposed laterite is smoothed and with an axe is cut into suitably sized blocks. (The special technique that is necessary for the cutting of laterite blocks must, it is thought, have been brought by the Khmers from India.) The quarried blocks are then shaped on the sides and bottom and exposed for a couple of days to sunlight, which hardens the blocks, and to the rain, which washes away the soft clay and leaves only the hardened laterite. In this way the Khmers obtained an extremely durable material for use in the framework of buildings and in the paving of roads.

Scholars are still debating the problem of where such huge supplies of laterite were obtained. Although it is widely dispersed throughout the region, no place has yet been discovered where it might have been quarried. According to one widely held theory, the laterite was taken from the canals and ponds that surrounded Angkor Wat and the other temples of the region. The theory is persuasive, but so far no adequate investigation has been made.

Sandstone, laid over the smooth surface of the laterite, was the noble material that was used for the carvings themselves; it was also used as roofing. Both blue and red sandstone are to be found, but with the one exception of Banteay Srei, blue stone was used exclusively. The reason was probably that it was considered more beautiful, although red stone, having a smaller iron content, is more resistant to wind and rain. That is why the buildings of Banteay Srei are so well preserved. Phnom Krom, atop a high hill, has been especially badly ravaged by the elements. Happily, Angkor Wat has not suffered the same fate, and its carvings are comparatively well preserved. Blocks of sandstone have no visible joints, being used without binding material, although it is surmised that iron shafts were inserted at strategic points.

The question of where this sandstone was quarried, like that of the laterite, has as yet no final answer, although there is a theory that the sandstone was found in the rocky district of Korat in Thailand and transported by boat to Angkor. This idea presupposes the existence of a canal at that time. Since the greater part of the mighty Khmer kingdom was composed of wide, flat plains, it is not unrea-

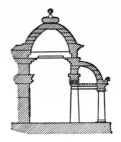

sonable to conclude that the sandstone did indeed come all the way by boat from the Korat region.

To get some idea of the way in which these materials were used, let us look for a moment at Angkor Wat, which combines two methods of construction: the lintel and the corbeled arch. The former was used over doorways, windows, and corridors and consisted merely of blocks of sandstone placed horizontally over pillars. The method is similar to that used in the construction of wooden buildings.

The corbeled arch was used for temple roofs and corridor widths. As shown in Figure 1, the method consisted of piling slabs of sandstone one upon the other from both left and right, completing the arch at the top. This method, which is fundamentally different from that employed by European architects for the construction of arches and vaults, was widely used in the Orient. It did not, because of its very nature, permit the construction of long arches such as are found in European buildings, although it did allow wider spans than the lintel.

Studies made of the corridors of Angkor Wat and other temples indicate that the outer limit of the corbeled arch was about sixteen feet; a different method had to be employed, therefore, for the construction of wider corridors and temples. Referring to Figure 1, we see that in order to broaden the interior space, another row of pillars was erected on one side, forming the basis for construction of an additional half-arch. In this manner the roof becomes two staged; the peculiar roof form of the corridor of Angkor Wat was born out of structural necessity. The horizontal beam connecting the inside and outside pillars helps strengthen the building.

Should a still wider space be needed—as, for example, in the cross-shaped third corridor of Angkor Wat—two rows of pillars must be constructed on either side and an extra corridor must also be created. This type of construction was used not only for corridors but also for dancing halls.

The tower is exceptional. Here blocks of stone were piled, one upon the other, from the four sides and made to meet in the center. In studying the towers, we find it truly amazing that the Khmers, building in an age when nothing resembling modern machinery was available to them, were yet able to elevate and heap huge blocks of stone to unbelievable heights in constructing their temples.

Although most extant buildings were constructed of laterite and sandstone, the Khmers, in the early period of their architectural development, also made use of bricks. In Icanapura, the ancient seventh-century capital, the buildings are composed of brick, and stone is used only for the lintels. (Brick, obviously, does not withstand the ravages of time as well as stone.) In the Roluos group, some twelve miles southeast of Angkor Wat, Prah Ko (879) and Lolei (893) are made of brick, as are both the East Mebon (952) and Pre Rup (961) in Angkor. However, Ta Keo, which was built toward the close of the tenth century and which adopts the same five-towered architectural style as East Mebon and Pre Rup, is constructed of stone. The switch from brick to stone seems to have taken place during the tenth century.

While corbeled arches could be constructed out of brick, lintels could only be made of stone; this also applies to wall carvings. Stucco, however, was used to create decorative wall patterns, and a number of designs in stucco are still to be seen on the brick walls of Prah Ko. Arabesque ornaments were created by the same method as in stone buildings.

ANGKOR WAT 卐

Wood also was used for the construction of buildings, such as royal palaces. Included among the carvings on the walls of the Bayon are a number of houses, but it is difficult to surmise, from carvings, what the houses must have looked like. The triangular sandstone gables of Banteay Srei, however, give the impression that wooden gables may have been copied exactly. The West Mebon, which is thought to have been built in the middle of the eleventh century, also retains vestiges of a wooden tower in the center. It seems quite probable that in earlier times wooden towers were frequently built, but through lack of evidence it is impossible to surmise what architectural style may have been used in the construction of these wooden towers.

EXTERIORS OF KHMER BUILDINGS

In Angkor Wat, as in all Khmer architecture, the tower constitutes the chief exterior feature. Looking at the central section of Angkor Wat from the long east-west sacred avenue, one sees cone-shaped towers soaring into the sky: a high central tower with four lesser towers on both right and left. The whole effect of the temple exterior resembles an isosceles triangle and suggests a geometrical composition at two and three levels.

The shape of the tower—which, seen from afar, looks not unlike an artillery shell—is uniquely Khmer. The composition of the tower is actually a square, the four corners of which are tiered, while the corners of the tiers have been cut away. Horizontal lines divide the tower into five to seven sections, and the tip of the tower assumes the form of a cone. On the horizontal sections, beside the borders, are a number of triangular-shaped spaces on which are carved *nagas* (stylized cobras) and *garudas* (birds with human bodies). Both *nagas* and *garudas* appear frequently in Khmer decoration; the *naga* particularly is intimately related to the stepped style of Khmer architecture.

Not all Khmer towers resemble those of Angkor Wat. Over the five gates of the Bayon and Angkor Thom stand four-faced towers of rather grotesque appearance, and relatively simply shaped brick towers are also to be found. However, the towers of Angkor Wat are the most refined in style of all Khmer towers and (excluding the exceptional four-faced towers) are also the most characteristic.

Although the ground plan of the Angkor Wat-type tower may be found in Indian architecture, the stepped style is nonexistent there. What, then, is the source of this unique form of tower? One opinion is that its origin may be traced to the *sikharas* (temple towers) of Hinduism. The curves of the shell-shaped tower of the Khmers resemble to a certain degree those of the *sikharas* of the Aryan style as well as the *sikharas* of Chalakyan and Dravidian style. The shape of the Khmer tower is, however, enormously different from that of the *sikharas*, but since the towered temple concept was certainly derived from the *sikharas*, it seems reasonable to conclude that the Khmer tower shape also was patterned after this same source.

The question then arises as to whether the tower was an original Khmer conception or whether it was influenced by foreign ideas. One theory holds that the tower represents the linga, which was one of the forms of the god Shiva. The theory is an attractive one because Shiva worship was very powerful in the region, but at the same time it is not wholly acceptable because not all Khmer towers resemble the linga in form. The square composition of the tower, with tiered surfaces, is not indigenously Khmer but is to be found frequently in Indian architecture, suggesting naturally that this method of tower construction derived originally from India. Borobudur of Java is another good example of the Indian method of construction, indicating that it is a type of tower found in countries that came under Indian architectural influence.

Division of the tower into horizontal sections also exists in the *sikharas* of India, but the numerous angles to be found on each section of a Khmer tower are apparently an original Khmer contribution. This same style may be found in towers erected in Champa, to the east of Cambodia. For instance, the tower near Quinhon, which was built around the eleventh or twelfth century, has angles on every section, although the surface is a square and closely resembles that of the towers of Angkor Wat. Though they were frequently at war, Champa and Cambodia also maintained trade and other relations, so it is hardly surprising that the architectural styles of both countries should possess certain similarities. The precise nature of these similarities is yet to be defined, since Champa architecture has been insufficiently studied.

The beautiful cone-shaped curves of the towers of Angkor Wat must have required a great deal of time to achieve. The narrowing of the brick tower of Prah Ko (879) seems fairly straight, but because damage to the structure is so severe, its overall shape is difficult to grasp. At Banteay Srei (967), however, which is made of red sandstone and is well preserved, the beginning of the cone-shaped tower may be seen. The straight lines of Prah Ko are even more apparent, and the narrowing of the tower, as it rises, is extreme. Horizontal lines are wider and more rugged. Ta Keo, which dates from a still later period, has been left unfinished. Of an even more rugged appearance, had it been completed, it would have possessed an exterior much like that of Banteay Srei.

The refined, typically Khmer towers of Angkor Wat exerted an influence on Thai architecture, which made itself felt when the Thais captured Angkor and began to copy its magnificent buildings. The Phra-Prang tower of present-day Thailand is doubtless designed after Khmer originals, as is the highly characteristic tower of Wat Arun, on the banks of the Menam. The only differences are that the angles of the various sections are much more highly developed and that vertical lines are more strongly emphasized than horizontal ones. The Thai tower is shorter, and at the same time the base is considerably broader, thus constituting a distinctive Thai style, despite obvious Khmer influence.

Another remarkable characteristic of Khmer architecture is the decoration of the gable. The somewhat bizarre appearance of Angkor Wat may be ascribed, at least in part, to its gables; Khmer gables have contributed greatly to the impressive nature of the architectural style. Since the roof of a Khmer structure is designed to meet at the center on sandstone slabs laid out horizontally from left to right, the cross section of the roof must be hidden at the eaves; this role is played by the distinctive Khmer gable.

Outwardly, the gables of Angkor Wat assume the form of stems undulating like the spikes of a crown from which leaves spiral out like wings. This makes the shape of the gable extremely complex. The stems are twisted and divided by a series of parallel lines, each of which is decorated with a pointlike pattern, suggesting the scaly body of a snake. This style of decoration, as it appears in ancient lintel carvings, was originally patterned after stems but later came to represent the bodies of serpents. At the bottommost point of the stems, which spread to both right and left, are carved *makaras*, sea monsters with the heads of elephants and gaping mouths that reveal enormous fangs. Out of these great mouths come seven-headed *nagas* that form the two edges of the gable.

The interior walls of the gables are richly decorated. The carvings are of two styles: one, which is quite free, tells a story; the other is geometrical. The lower part is separated into one, two, or three sections, divided without the use of lines, and a sitting figure is carved in each section. In the upper part, which corresponds to the top of the crown, the principal carved figures are set in geometrical patterns. The Bayon adopts this geometrical arrangement for the Buddha figures.

Even more curious are the numerous instances in which the gables stand one on top of the other. At the entrance of a building, for example, the gable over the roof of the porch and that on top of the passage overlap, while the gables over the roofs of the stairs also overlap one another in several tiers. The further fact that the passage has a subcorridor and a two-tiered roof makes the exterior appearance of the gables even more complex. At times the *naga* with raised head at the edge of the gable gives the impression of a flame, at other times of a petal, in either case rendering the roof more beautiful.

The study of the development of the curious decorations of Khmer gables is inhibited by the fact that nothing remains of seventh- and eighth-century brick buildings to reveal their decorative style. It seems likely that the gables of those early days were ornamented with stucco figures, and although their style is not known, the decorations may have taken the shape of an inverted U or horseshoe.

The remains of a Cambodian building called Damrei Krap, thought to have been constructed at the beginning of the ninth century, demonstrate remarkable advances over the simple U-shaped decorations, presaging the soft, curved lines of the future. Curled-leaf ornamentation is to be seen at the edges of the gable, which is rather high and similar in proportion to the gables of Hindu temples in Champa, revealing the close relationship between the two styles. This early ninth-century Khmer gable has, however, been damaged to such an extent that it is impossible to make any more detailed assumptions about it.

During the tenth century, Cambodian gables began to be made of sandstone and so have come down to us in a far better state of preservation. At Prah Ko, for example, we see carvings of *makaras* with gaping mouths on both edges of the gable, showing Javanese influence, and on the small wall within the gable are arabesques carved around the central figures of the gods, with numerous carvings of lesser gods within the curlicues. The inspiration for most of these carvings comes from the vegetable kingdom, thus differing from the gable carvings of Angkor Wat.

Around the time of the completion of Banteay Srei (967), the art of gable decoration made remarkable advances, resulting in the finest known examples of this type. Wide, thorny stems twist and curl, and in the middle of the stems are rows of flowers. The overall effect is rather flat, giving the impression of the body of a snake. Although the ornamentation is not as fine as that at Angkor Wat, it is richer in strong, daring curves that form lovely patterns. The ornamentation of the gables, taking its inspiration entirely from vegetation, is both flamboyant and elegant.

This style, which reached its height around this period, is pre-

ANGKOR WAT 🈁

sent in all its glory at Angkor Wat, although by that time the technique had deteriorated somewhat. In some eleventh-century gables, the head of the *makara* has disappeared, with the result that the curves form the body of the *naga* directly. It was probably around this time that the stems of leaves were formed with the deliberate intention of representing the body of the *naga*. Then, in the twelfth-century gables of Angkor Wat, the hideous figure of the *makara* makes its debut, but the stems continue to express, as before, the bodies of snakes.

An important feature in the stepped composition of the structures is the fact that the roofs of the corridors are half-cylinders, like a Quonset hut. This is especially true of Angkor Wat, where triple corridors are arranged in pyramidal form: a distant view gives the impression that the roofs are piled one upon the other, in several layers. At first glance, this rounded roof is reminiscent of the Japanese tiled roof, with indentations on its surface. Tiles with comma-shaped decoration (like those on Japanese tiled roofs) are to be found at the edges of the eaves; in fact, they are seven-headed *nagas*, with the knobs on the surface of the roof representing the body of the serpent. Thus, the influence of *naga* worship is apparent even in small details, enhancing the idiosyncracy of the ornamentation.

DECORATIVE ELEMENTS IN KHMER ARCHITECTURE

Khmer buildings of Indian inspiration (including Angkor Wat) are decorated in a complex, elegant, and even voluptuous fashion, but the decoration is never, as is frequently the case in India, pornographic. Surprisingly, a number of Khmer decorative elements are not of Indian inspiration. Some students believe that these non-

Indian elements are purely the products of Khmer creativity, but this assertion is questionable, since Occidental forms and highly Oriental Chinese forms exist side by side. This fact seems to offer sufficient proof that the forms are not native Khmer in origin but are the result of foreign influences.

Ornamental patterns that are Western in type appear on pilasters, false doors, and lintels: these are leaf-shaped and include spiraling small leaves, in the center of which are depicted figures of gods and human beings and the heads of monstrous animals. The fact that some of the leaves closely resemble the acanthus, as it was used in Greece and Rome, might seem coincidental, with no relationship to classical Western art, but this would be a rather simplistic judgment, since Roman-type arabesques based on the curled leaf are found on the pillars of such buildings as Prah Ko and Bakon Lolei.

At the point where the leaf is about to curl there are ring-shaped leaves where a lotus flower has been introduced in order to fill the space thus created. It may be regarded as the same lotus flower found in Assyrian art, which is the fountainhead of classical Western art. The decorative elements of Prah Ko (considered to be the prototype of chevron-shaped ornamentation frequently found on Khmer pillars) consist of a central stem with a calyx above, and over it a lotus flower with petals and stamen supported by flame-shaped leaves.

In attempting to determine the origin of the curled-leaf type of ornamentation found at Angkor Wat, as well as in other buildings, examples exist that suggest classical Western influence far too strongly to be dismissed as mere coincidence. Historically, we know that in the third century not only Indians and Persians but people

ANGKOR WAT 圀

from the Roman territories of the East arrived by boat in what is now Canton on the Chinese mainland. We also know that these people stopped at ports in both the Khmer kingdom and in Champa on their way to and from Canton. Given these circumstances, it is hardly surprising that Western culture found its way into the two countries. As a matter of fact, ornamentation patterned after West Asian styles may be found in present-day Java. We may safely assert that cultural interchange took place between West Asia and Southeast Asia, but since Western elements have not been found in decoration antedating the ninth century, further studies must determine whether Western influence was direct or indirect.

In any consideration of Western influence, the shapes of Khmer pillars must also be taken into account. Several types of pillars are to be found at Angkor Wat, including the square independent pillar, the pilaster, and the multifoil column. The former two are of such similar shape that they may be considered to be of the same type. The first, the square independent pillar, was used in corridors and also in porches, in front of entrances and exits, while the second, the pilaster, was used in front of porch walls diametrically opposite the independent pillar and also on either side of open entrances.

Both the capital and base of the square pillar had a fixed style, although the base was frequently omitted in corridor pillars, while the capital was similar in form to that of the Corinthian pilaster of classical Rome. This similarity is rarely encountered elsewhere in the Orient, even in India. Ornamentation is somewhat richer than in the Roman counterpart, and decorative themes are not the same. Acanthus leaves, for example, furnish the inspiration for the Roman capital, whereas the ornamentation of Angkor Wat makes use of lotuslike petals. On the upper part of the rectangular slab, a row of round, eight-petalled flowers is carved on all four sides. Thus we see that while the shape of the square pillar is Western, the mood created by the decorative themes is strongly Oriental.

The pillar is not fluted, and its decoration seems to depend on its importance in the overall architectural scheme: some pillars are not decorated at all, in some the arris is decorated, and in others the decoration appears below the central line of the pillar. The pillars in the colonnade of the first corridor have no bases but spring directly from the floor. Inscribed on the lower section is a form resembling a pointed arch, within which are carved kneeling gods, while the upper part bears a number of horizontal bands making use of floral ornamentation.

Base decorations are in extremely low relief, giving them an Oriental flavor. Another characteristic of this type of pillar is that the surface is relatively flat. The pillar displays virtually no Indian elements at all; it is Western in form and Eastern in ornamental themes.

Decorative elements at Angkor Wat that make use of Oriental themes may also be seen on the frameworks of windows and entranceways, as well as on sections of the walls. Where Occidental-style patterns seem more sculptural, those of the Oriental type are flat and in extremely low relief. Forms used include round patterns, arabesque round patterns, and two interlaced circles; the designs vary depending on their position—whether they appear on windows or in entranceways—but in either case they demonstrate a rich inventive genius.

The chief inspiration for the round pattern is derived from the world of plants, as is that of the freely arranged arabesques. These arabesque patterns are similar to certain patterns used by the Japa-

ANGKOR WAT 畢

nese in dyeing cloth, and it is interesting to conjecture a common source, especially since both share the pattern of two interlaced circles.

In any study of the development of Oriental ornamental patterns, the close and ancient relationship between Cambodia and China must be taken into consideration. As far back as the year 616, Khmer emissaries brought tribute to China and returned to Cambodia bearing gifts of cloth from the Chinese emperor. Inevitably, Khmers who had the opportunity of seeing this cloth must have been influenced by its designs when they set about creating their own patterns. Angkor Wat abounds in ornamentation of this type, while only a few rather coarse elements suggesting Chinese influence are to be found in the Bayon. One authority suggests that Chinese architects must have taken part in the construction of Angkor Wat, but there is no concrete evidence to support his theory.

On the outer wall of the third corridor of Angkor Wat, as well as on the outer wall of the library situated between the third and second corridors, are checkerboard squares containing human figures shown amidst petal-shaped designs resembling round patterns and surrounded by arabesques. The squares, which look rather as though sculptured tiles had been attached to the walls, are extremely Oriental in mood. This particular type of ornamentation is older than Angkor Wat, being found on the outer wall of the prayer hall in front of the central temple of Banteay Srei (967). In the latter, however, both the vertical and the horizontal lattices are more deeply carved, and within the squares floral and curled-leaf designs are found. Although the Oriental mood is not so pervasive here as in Angkor Wat, it is significant that the flat lattice-type division is unknown in India.

In conclusion, a brief word may be said on the relationship between Khmer and Javanese decorative elements. Since the architecture of both countries is of Indian origin, it is only to be expected that there should be a close connection between them. Setting this aside, however, there is evidence that Khmer architecture was directly influenced by Java—evidence that was brought to light when the ruins of Phnom Kulen were excavated in 1936. Lintel carvings depicted both *kalas* and *makaras*, monsters frequently encountered in Javanese sculpture. Further Javanese influence is to be found, to a certain degree, in the shape of Khmer towers. A good example of this is the group of lesser towers surrounding the five towers of Phnom Bakheng. Their extreme simplicity suggests Javanese influence, but this influence decreases as the years pass and Khmer architecture comes into its own. Very little Javanese influence, for example, is apparent at Angkor Wat. It was exerted directly from the first half of the ninth century until the second half of the tenth century, while during the twelfth century, when Angkor Wat was being built, native Khmer architecture had advanced to such an extent that only the slightest vestiges of Javanese influence are still apparent.

ANGKOR WAT 囷

NOTES TO THE PLATES

1. Standing atop the hill crowned by Phnom Bakheng (which is thought to have been constructed by King Yasovarman) and looking toward the east, the visitor is rewarded with a magnificent view of Angkor Wat and its five towers soaring over the luxuriant jungle. Because Angkor Wat was never buried by jungle growth and because people continued throughout the years to pray at the temple, the building remains relatively well preserved; its scale is the largest of all Khmer ruins. On the far horizon lies the vast plain of Cambodia.

2. Of Angkor Wat's four Gopurams (tower gates), facing each of the four directions, the widest is that on the west; the south gate, shown in this plate, is situated at the end of the broad road that leads northward from Siem Reap. Behind the gate rises a tower whose form is typically Khmer. These tower gates were not merely entrances and exits but were special sacred buildings in themselves, with images of the gods and of the Buddha enshrined in some of them.

3. Over the west Gopuram (257 yards wide) stand three towers, typically Khmer in form. Although the tops of the towers have vanished, the interiors still retain images of the gods, and the wall decorations are considered to be particularly beautiful. Angkor Wat was constructed during the first half of the twelfth century.

4. This first corridor on the west side of Angkor Wat is raised some thirteen feet above the ground; the sides of the platform are decorated with moldings and ornamental carvings. The central

part of the corridor lies to the left of the photograph, while in the foreground may be glimpsed the long colonnaded corridor itself.

5. After entering through the west tower gate, the visitor comes upon a sacred road, paved with stones, which is 10 yards wide and runs in a perfectly straight line for 519 yards. At its end stands a great temple. The first corridor is 197 yards long from north to south and 235 yards from east to west.

6. The wall reliefs of Angkor Wat's first corridor are especially well known for their beauty; all are of a religious nature and were clearly intended to instruct the people on doctrinal matters. Originally the reliefs were covered with gold leaf over a lacquer base, gilding the whole corridor.

7. *Devatas* (goddesses) in low relief decorate the inner wall of Angkor Wat's second corridor. Faces, bodies, and hands of the goddesses are all frontal, while their feet point sideways; the reliefs may have been produced at a time before the technique of drawing was perfected. The mouths of the *devatas* suggest typically Khmer features.

8. The third corridor of Angkor Wat stands on a platform fourteen yards high, with a particularly handsome overlapping molding. The fact that the stone steps are so steep the visitor must literally crawl up them on hands and knees suggests that this corridor must have been forbidden to commoners.

9. The central gate of Angkor Wat's west facade, along with the high platform of the third corridor, is most impressive. In the background soars the central tower. The third corridor, on its

high platform, is in the foreground; the building on the left is the library, situated between the second and third corridors, on whose walls may be seen the *devatas* in low relief; and above the library rises the tower at the northwest corner of the third corridor.

10. On climbing the third corridor and looking west, the visitor sees the west Gopuram in the foreground and the sacred road beyond the second corridor. To the right is the central gate of the second corridor; in front stands the isolated library. The gable over the gate is highly characteristic of Khmer architecture.

11. The third corridor, which stands fourteen yards above the inner yard of the second corridor, is composed of sixty-six-yard-long sections. On each of its four sides are three wide staircases, each with forty steps. The central staircase rises to a cross-shaped corridor, which leads in turn to the central temple. The other stairways of the third corridor lead to its corner towers.

12. In the inner court of the first and second corridors were facilities for ablutions. At the right of the building may be seen a section of the corridor that connects the first and second corridors. The overlapping gable is an interesting example of Khmer architectural style.

13-14. Angkor Thom, which was built toward the end of the twelfth century, possesses a total of five gates—four central gates and the Victory Gate on the east side. They are all similarly shaped and atop all of them stands the four-faced tower of Lokeshvara, a motif of which Jayavarman VII, a Buddhist king, seems to have been especially fond. Shown here are two views of the south gate. In Plate 14, in front of the gate, the balustrades of the bridge across the canal are composed of giants more than six feet tall carrying the bodies of *nagas*. This theme is believed to have been taken from the wall reliefs of Angkor Wat's first corridor, where the churning of the sea of milk is depicted.

15.   The Bayon, which stands at the precise geometrical center of Angkor Thom, is a Buddhist temple built around the end of the twelfth century. It is the last of the great monuments of Khmer architecture. It measures 175 yards from east to west and 153 yards from north to south. The principal entrance faces east; here there originally stood a terrace decorated with lions and *nagas*.

16.   The outer corridor of the Bayon was badly damaged at the time of the Thai invasion, and the roof has fallen in. The total length of the outer corridor and the complex inner corridor is 1,320 yards. Shown in this plate is the south entrance to the outer corridor. It was rectangular in shape and divided into eight distinct sections, with small chapels standing at its four corners and also at the center of the four sides of the rectangle. On the lintel in the background may be seen reliefs of *apsaras* (celestial dancers), while on either side of the entrance stand figurs of *dvarapalas* (guardians of the temple) holding staffs in their hands.

17.   The scenes depicted in relief on the walls of the outer corridor of the Bayon are taken from Khmer history and from the everyday life of the people rather than from religious sources. Such scenes of battles and of ordinary daily life furnish invaluable information about the existence of the people at the time the Bayon was built, during the second half of the twelfth century. The laws of perspective being then unknown, distance is shown by the position of the relief.

ANGKOR WAT 閣

18.   The third story of the Bayon consists of a cross-shaped terrace on which stand twenty towers. In the background, to the right, may be seen the great central temple. At the time the terrace was discovered, it lay buried beneath giant trees, which, Pierre Loti wrote in his *Pèlerin d'Angkor*, made it a dark and terrifying place.

19.   The large tower seen at the left of this photograph is the central temple, while on the surrounding twenty towers of the terrace are carved the four-faced figures of Lokeshvara (the Compassionate Boddhisattva). In every case, the corners of the mouth are turned slightly up, suggesting a smile. This group of towers constitutes an architectural marvel unrivaled anywhere else in the world.

20–21.   At first the Bayon was thought to have been built by Yasovarman as a central pedestal, and the four-faced figures were assumed to represent Brahma. But more recent studies have made it clear that the Bayon was a Buddhist temple constructed by Jayavarman VII and that the figures must therefore be intended to represent Lokeshvara. Pierre Loti said his blood curdled as he saw huge face after huge face, each smiling endlessly down at him.

22.   Within the irregular corridor that surrounds the Bayon's cross-shaped terrace stands a small building. The window shown in the wall is a false one, with a level surface above, upon which, originally, it is thought, reliefs were carved in stucco. Today, on either side of the window, stands an image of a *devata*.

23–24.   The Terrace of the Elephants, which was constructed in the latter half of the twelfth century, derives its name from the herds of elephants carved on the wide walls between the extensions of the terrace. Plate 23 shows one of these extensions, where the *garuda* and the lion, both with human bodies, support the terrace. In Plate 24 is seen a corner of one of the extensions, or protruding platforms, being supported by the trunk of an elephant—a repetition of a motif found in a corner of an Angkor Thom gate.

25–26.   On the terrace, which measures 273 yards in length, were conference halls, court rooms, and reception halls; the terrace was situated east of the walls surrounding the Royal Palace and facing the main square. The elephant herd is seen in Plate 25, while Plate 26 shows the lions that border the extension stairs. With gaping mouths, and staring up into the sky, the figures are good examples of Khmer sculptural style.

27.   The Terrace of the Leper King, which was constructed around the same time as the Terrace of the Elephants, lies somewhat to the north of it. It takes its name from a seated figure in the innermost recess of the terrace who, according to legend, represents King Yasovarman, the founder of Angkor. Yasovarman is said to have died of leprosy; but both suppositions seem to be little more than legend, with no hard evidence to substantiate them. The wall carvings, which are quite different from those on the Terrace of the Elephants, depict for the most part a monarch, surrounded by nobles and concubines, engaged in court ceremonies.

28.   The Phimeanakas, which stands at the center of the area enclosed by the walls of the Royal Palace, was built at the beginning of the eleventh century by Rajendravarman II, as his main building, when he brought the capital of the country back from Koh Ker to Angkor. The pyramidal platform rests on a base that is thirty-

ANGKOR WAT 米

eight yards in length from east to west, thirty-one yards from north to south, and thirteen yards high.

29.　The Prah Palilay, which was built during the second half of the twelfth century, lies in the square north of the Royal Palace, beyond the wooden foundation of the Tep Pranam, a Buddhist monastery. The base of the tower is four-tiered, but the stone blocks used in the construction of the tower have fallen, and only the central chimney section remains.

30.　The Prasat Suor Prat are twelve high laterite towers, erected toward the end of the tenth century, which stand in front of the north and south halls (called Kleangs) rather as though they were guards of honor. According to legend, acrobats once performed upon tight leather ropes stretched from tower to tower; the Prasat Suor Prat are therefore known as the Towers of the Tight-rope Walkers. There is nothing to substantiate this legend, and the real purpose of the towers remains so far unknown.

31.　The Baksei Chamkrong is situated near the south gate of Angkor Thom and is clearly seen, on the left, from the road leading to the gate. The tower, which was erected at the beginning of the tenth century, attains a height of thirteen yards. On the base of the tower is an inscription that reads: "In the reign of Rajendravarman II, 947," At one time the Prasat is thought to have enshrined a golden image of Shiva. The small surrounding wall and the east tower gate are now in ruins.

32–33.　Phnom Bakheng is the central edifice of the Angkor that was constructed toward the end of the ninth century by King Yasovarman. It stands near the south gate of Angkor Thom, on a hill adjacent to the Baksei Chamkrong. Plate 32 shows a view of the east side of Phnom Bakheng's man-made mound, which rises to a height of seventy-one yards and supports five towers on a pyramidal base made of sandstone. Beneath this base is a five-tiered pyramid nine yards high; it is seventy-nine yards square at the bottom and forty-four yards square at the top; on the five tiers are a total of forty-five small towers. In Plate 33 is shown the central tower.

34.   Phnom Krom rises some seven miles southeast of Siem Reap and overlooks the great lake, Tonle Sap. Standing atop the hill (*phnom*) are three towers, in which the three supreme Hindu gods were enshrined: Shiva in the center, Vishnu in the north tower, and Brahma in the south. The Brahma figure is still to be seen in the south tower, but because of their location on top of an exposed hill, the towers have been much damaged by the elements.

35.   Prah Khan, located to the north of Angkor Thom, is a Buddhist temple constructed in 1191 by King Jayavarman VII. It is surrounded by a high laterite wall whose dimensions are 700 yards from north to south and 897 yards from east to west. A gate opens in the center of each wall, and along the wall is a moat spanned by a bridge depicting Deva and Asura carrying the double *naga* of the churning scene.

36–38.   The central section of Prah Khan is encircled by two enclosures, that which contains the central temple running sixty-one yards from east to west and fifty-nine yards from north to south. There are also a number of smaller temples, which, although they lack the splendor of Angkor Wat, represent the last great flowering of Khmer architecture. Plate 37 shows the end of Prah Khan's balustrade, which takes the form of a *naga* hovered over by images of the *garuda*, the legendary bird that Vishnu is said to have ridden and whose favorite food was snakes. (The *garuda* is now the national emblem of Thailand.) In Plate 38 may be seen the west entrance to Prah Khan's second enclosure. On either side stand small pillars supporting the lintel and larger round pillars holding up the gable above. This arrangement is common to Khmer architecture, with differences in form and style depending on the period in which the structure was built.

39–40.　Prah Neak Pean was built in the latter part of the twelfth century on a small island in the center of a large lake that no longer exists today; it lies to the east of Prah Khan. On a seven-tiered base, with two *nagas* circling the round part of the base, rises a central tower dedicated to Lokeshvara. Around the tower there was once a number of animal figures, but the animals on three sides have vanished with the passing of the years, leaving only the figure of a huge horse on the east side. A group of men may be seen clinging to the figure.

41.　Pre Rup (961) lies south of the East Mebon, on the curve of Angkor's "main circuit," as it is called. On a pyramidal base stand five brick towers, with stone decorations around the entranceways. The central terrace is about thirty-three yards square and some sixteen yards high.

42.　East Mebon was built in 912 by Rajendravarman II on an island in the center of the great lake constructed by Yasovarman. Built a few years earlier than the Pre Rup, it is very similar to it, although its pyramidal base is slightly lower. Its brick tower was originally covered with stucco ornamentation.

43. In front of the east gate of the Banteay Kedei is a handsome lake called Srah Srang, and here, at the end of the twelfth century, Jayavarman VII constructed a fine terrace. The dimensions of the lake are 875 yards from east to west and 437 yards from north to south. The bottom of the lake is paved with stone, and laterite steps have been built around it. It was used by high priests.

44–46. Banteay Kedei, constructed toward the end of the twelfth century, lies to the west of Srah Srang and is similar in every respect to the nearby temple of Ta Prohm. In Plate 44 we see the Gopuram (tower gate) of the second enclosure after having made our way through the east entrance. This Gopuram could never have been a mere entranceway, since even today three seated images are to be found in it. Another view of the east gate is shown in Plate 46. Here, in the inner recess of the pillared porch, stands a building with a cross-shaped ground plan. The window is bordered by niches enshrining Buddhist images. In Plate 45 are seen sculptured figures of the ubiquitous *apsaras*, or celestial dancers; these appear on many Angkor pillars, and most especially on pillars in dancing halls. In general, both the architecture and the ornamentation of Banteay Kedei are of poor quality—due, perhaps, to the late date of its construction.

47. Ta Prohm (1186), situated to the east of Angkor Thom, is an important Buddhist temple and a splendid example of Khmer architectural greatness. It has been preserved as it was when it was first found, obscured by the jungle's enormous trees, whose huge

roots seem to twist about the structure like writhing serpents.

48.   Ta Keo, which is to be found to the east of Angkor Thom's
Gate of Victory, is typical of a Khmer five-towered temple standing
on a pyramidal base. Sacred to Shiva, it was begun by Jayavarman
V, who supervised the erection of its huge blocks of stone, but the
temple itself was never completed. Had it been, it would surely have
ranked as one of Angkor's finest monuments.

49.   Erected in the later half of the twelfth century, Ta Nei (which
lies to the north of Ta Keo, at the northwest corner of the eastern
lake) is considered to be representative of the architectural style of
buildings constructed during the reign of Jayavarman VII. Shown
in Plate 49 is one of two kinds of Khmer gable: in this the figures
are carved in orderly horizontal bands. In the other type of gable
the figures seem to be scattered helter-skelter over the surface of
the gable wall. The stems and leaves that formed the edges of the
gables gradually began, as Khmer architectural ornament progres-
sed, to resemble seven-headed *nagas* (but in this particular gable the
resemblance is obscure).

50–51.   The West Mebon, which dates from the latter part of the
eleventh century, is situated in the center of an artificial lake to the
west of Angkor Thom. In the past, people used to visit the temple,
departing from the west gate of Angkor Thom, either on elephant-
back or in carriages, but at the present time the level of the water
has risen so high that the temple may be reached only by boat.
According to ancient maps, the building was surrounded by a square
enclosure measuring seventy-one yards on each side, with three
gates in each of the four sides. On the central pedestal stood a wood-

en tower, which has now vanished; only the gates and parts of the walls remain. Plate 51 shows sections of the pillars that stand on either side of one of the gates; the pillars are divided into panels, into which curious figures of animals have been carved. This same type of decoration is also to be found in the Baphuon (which was built around the same time), but not in other Angkor temples.

52–53. The visitor to the West Mebon must take a half-hour boat ride across the western *baray*, a man-made lake or reservoir, which is slightly larger in area than the eastern *baray*. Since the level of the water of the west lake has risen in recent years, only the tops of the trees in the eastern part of the lake are visible, the trunks and lower leaves being submerged.

54–59. Banteay Srei, erected in 967 about twelve miles to the northeast of Angkor, is dedicated to the god Shiva. Although the scale of the temple is not remarkably large, it is famous for its sculpture, which represents Khmer art at its highest level. The central section is surrounded by a triple enclosure with three towers. A detail of one tower is shown in Plate 58, indicating the depth of the carving and the boldness and sweep of the lines. The three towers are similarly constructed; the south tower, shown in Plate 54, is eight yards high and about three yards wide. Plate 55 gives a front view of the prayer hall, which stands before the central tower; the south and north towers may be seen to the right and left of the building. To reach the prayer hall, one passes through a small gate in the third enclosure. The small scale of the hall is indicated by the fact that its entrance, under a lintel, is only just over one yard high. The walls (shown in Plate 56) are patterned like a checkerboard and covered with floral decorations, imparting to the building

ANGKOR WAT 㻪

a strongly Oriental look. On either side of the entrance are monkey-faced figures. The gables of Banteay Srei are especially notable. That over the east gate of the second enclosure is shown in Plate 57. It is of the rare triangular form and retains vestiges of a wooden structure; both its line and its ornamentation are famous for their beauty. On either side of the road leading to this gate are linga-shaped images. The gable of the south tower may be seen in Plate 59; it is in the shape of an inverted U, with carvings on the lintel above the entranceway. Banteay Srei is a rare example of a temple made entirely of red sandstone, and since it has been little damaged by the wind and the rain of the passing centuries, the splendor of the carvings comes through with remarkable clarity. One leaves it with renewed respect for the artistic genius of the Khmers, a genius that was in every way equal to that of Java.

60. In order to visit Banteay Samre, one walks among palm trees and lush jungle plants and passes through an agreeable Cambodian village, with its houses raised high on stilts. The temple is enclosed by a laterite wall that measures forty-eight yards from east to west and thirty-eight yards from north to south, with an inner corridor. In front of the central temple is a prayer hall, with a library on either side of the hall. The temple, judging by the architectural style, was probably erected during the Angkor Wat period.

61. Bakong, one of the so-called Roluos group, stands some twelve miles to the southeast of Angkor Wat. Constructed by King Indra-varman I in 881, Bakong was the central temple of the pre-Angkor capital of Hariharalaya. Standing on a pyramidal base, the original temple was built of wood.

62–63.   Prah Ko, also in the Roluos group, was built during the same reign and stands to the north of Bakong. The central section has six towers made entirely of brick except for a few stone details; the brick was then covered with stucco ornamentation, some of which still remains to provide interesting information about the period. This is an ancient method of construction that antedates the use of sandstone, although stone niches may be seen in the detail shown in Plate 63.

64.   Lolei, another member of the Roluos group, was built in 893 on a small islet in the middle of the large reservoir that provided water for Indravarman's capital of Hariharalaya. In this it resembles the Mebons of Angkor, save that the reservoir is now empty. Six towers were originally planned for the temple of Lolei, but only four were actually constructed.

65–66.   Cambodian houses are of simple structure, in part because of the hot climate, and are customarily raised on high stilts, which not only offer protection against flooding but also help keep the heat of the ground away from the floors of the houses. Plate 65 shows the view from the height of Phnom Krom, with the houses of the village built alongside the canals. In the far distance may be seen the great lake, Tonle Sap.

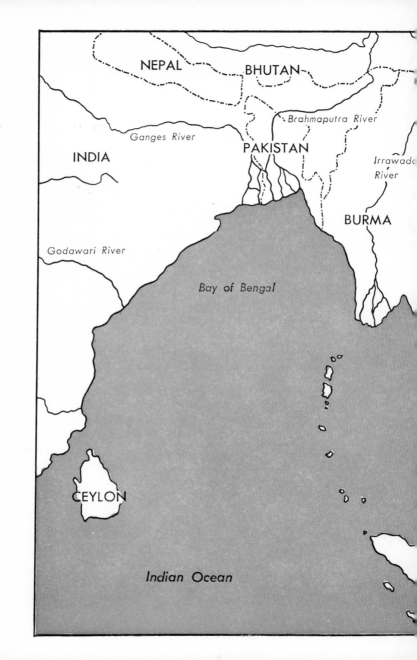

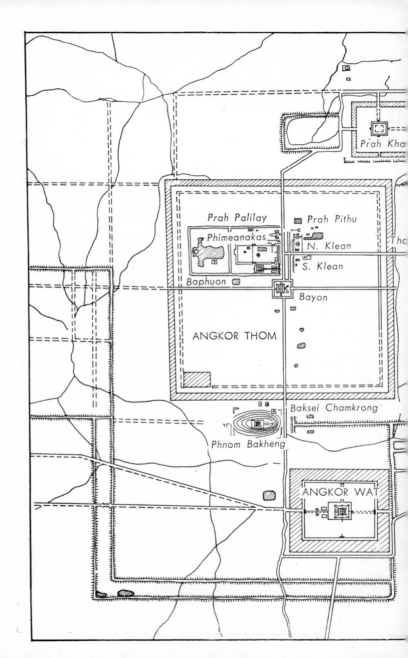

Prah Kha

Prah Palilay   Prah Pithu

Phimeanakas   N. Klean   The

S. Klean

Baphuon

Bayon

ANGKOR THOM

Baksei Chamkrong

Phnom Bakheng

ANGKOR WAT

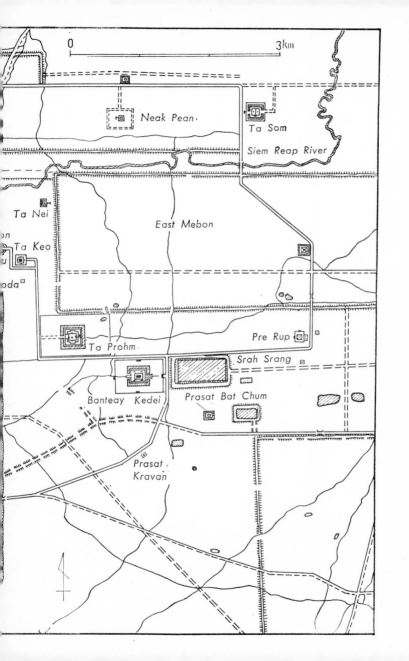

0   3km

Neak Pean·

Ta Som

Siem Reap River

Ta Nei

East Mebon

Ta Keo

oda□

Pre Rup

Ta Prohm·

Srah Srang

Banteay Kedei

Prasat Bat Chum

Prasat·
Kravan

1. *Angkor Wat*, built during the first half of the twelfth century, presents a splendid sight as seen from Phnom Bakheng.

2. *The South Gopuram* (tower gate) at Angkor Wat is one of four; these were not mere gates but were sacred structures enshrining holy images.

◄3. *The West Gopuram*, the widest of Angkor Wat's four, is considered to have especially beautiful wall decorations.

4. *The first corridor* of Angkor Wat stands well above the ground on an ornamental platform; shown here is the west side.

5. *The west facade* of Angkor Wat stands at the end of a sacred road that runs in a perfectly straight line for 520 yards.

6. *Wall reliefs* of the first corridor at Angkor Wat all derive their inspiration from religious themes.

8. *The third corridor* at Angkor Wat ▶
stands on a fourteen-yard-high platform; shown here is the west side.

7. *The second corridor* of Angkor Wat
is devoted to the depiction of *devatas*
(goddesses), whose features here are
thought to be typically Khmer.

9. *The central gate* in the west side of
Angkor Wat is considered to be one
of the building's chief glories.

10. *The view* to the west, from the
height of Angkor Wat's third corridor
shows many of the special features of
the structure.

11. *The third corridor* has a total of ▶
twelve stairways, each with forty
steps; the central stairway leads to the
main temple.

13-14. *The south gate* is one of five at Angkor Thom (end of the twelfth century); all are surmounted by the figure of the Compassionate Bodhisattva.

15. *The Bayon*, the last of
the great Khmer monu-
ments, was built during the
second half of the twelfth
century; seen here is the
east side.

16. *The outer corridor* of the Bayon, partly destroyed by the Thais, still has reliefs of dancers and temple guardians.

17. *Reliefs* on the east side of the Bayon's first corridor show battle scenes as well as scenes from the daily life of the people.

◀18. *The east terrace* of the Bayon supports twenty towers in addition to the central temple.

19. *The central temple* of the Bayon and the twenty surrounding towers are a unique architectural accomplishment.

20-21. *Lokeshvara* is supposed to be compassionate, but Pierre Loti found his unending smile terrifying.

22. *Statues of devatas* (goddesses) stand on either side of a false window in the Bayon.

23-24. *The Terrace of the Elephants*, east of the Palace walls, is 273 yards long, with three large projecting platforms. One of these, sustained by *garudas* and lions, is shown below; on the following page, the platform is seen being supported by the trunk of an elephant.

25-26. *A herd of elephants* (above) and standing lions (below) are both taken from the Terrace of the Elephants.

27. *The Terrace of the Leper King* takes its name from the enigmatic seated figure, which, according to legend, is that of Yasovarman, Angkor's founder.

29. *Prah Palilay*, built at the close of ▶
the twelfth century, has fallen into
ruin, and only the core of the central
tower remains standing.

28. *Phimeanakas*, an early eleventh-
century construction of Rajendravarman II: shown below is the northeast side.

31. *Baksei Chamkrong* is a tower thirteen yards high; on its base are inscribed the words: "In the reign of Rajendravarman II, 947." ►

30. *Prasat Suor Prat* were known to legend as the Towers of the Tightrope Walkers, but their true purpose is still to be discovered.

32-33. *Phnom Bakheng,* the central
point of Yasovarman's Angkor, was
erected at the end of the ninth century; opposite is a view from the
east side, while the plate below shows
the central tower.

34. *Phnom Krom*, dating from the beginning of the tenth century, has three towers, in the southernmost of which is an image of the Hindu god, Brahma.

35. *Prah Khan*, a Buddhist temple built in 1191, has balustrades of giants at the entrance to its walled enclosure.

36-38. *Other architectural features* of Prah Khan include its central section (below), the end of the balustrade, showing *nagas* and *garudas* (left), and the typically pillared west entrance to the second enclosure (opposite).

39-40. *Neak Pean*, built during the latter part of the twelfth century, once stood in the center of a large lake, (which has since disappeared); vanished also are its ornamental figures, save for the monumental horse shown below.

41. *Pre Rup*, with its five brick towers on a pyramidal base, as seen from the east.

42. *East Mebon*, although built almost twenty years earlier, bears a close resemblance to Pre Rup.

115

44. *Banteay Kedei* (end of twelfth century): the tower gate that faces the visitor after he makes his way through the east entrance.

45. *The apsaras* (heavenly dancers) of Banteay Kedei are typical of the dancing figures found on so many Khmer pillars.

46. *East Gate* of Banteay Kedei shows the relative poverty of the building's architecture and decoration, due perhaps to the late date of its construction.

47. *Ta Prohm* (erected in 1186) has been left in the overgrown state in which it was originally discovered.

48. *Prasat Ta Keo*, a five-towered temple sacred to the god Siva, was begun by Jayavarman V but was never finished.

49. *Ta Nei*, of the architectural style
of Jayavarman VII, possesses a gable
in which small figures are carved in
relief in numerous horizontal bands.

50. *West Mebon*, which may now be ▶
reached only by boat, has disappeared
into the past, save for its gates and
parts of its walls.

51. *The pilasters* that border one of the gates of the West Mebon have curious animal carvings.

52-53. *The Western*▶ *Lake* is higher than it used to be, and much of the half-hour boat ride to the West Mebon is shaded by the tops of submerged trees.

54-55. *Banteay Srei,* which lies about twelve miles northeast of Angkor, was built in 967 and is considered by scholars to be one of the finest examples of Khmer architecture and architectural decoration. Shown above is the south tower; opposite, the prayer hall in front of the central tower.

56. *The south side* of
the prayer hall, with
its checkerboard wall
decorated in Oriental
fashion with floral
carvings: figures with
monkey faces guard
the low entrance.

129

57. *The gable* over the enclosure is considered to be especially fine; its triangular shape is rare.

58. *Details* from the central tower of Banteay Srei show the high level of artistic skill and invention attained by Khmer sculptors.

59. *In the form* of an inverted U, the gable of the south tower has decorative sculpture on the lintel above the entranceway.

60. *Banteay Samre*: the central temple, with the prayer hall in front; constructed probably in the first half of the twelfth century.

61. *Bakong*, of the early Roluos group, was built in the year 881 by King Indravarman I.

62. *Prah Ko*, north of Bakong, was also built during the reign of Indravaraman; the three towers in the foreground were dedicated to Shiva.

63. *The brick tower* of Prah Ko was constructed before the use of sandstone.

64. *Lolei* originally stood in the center of a reservoir that served the pre-Angkor capital; the reservoir is now empty.▶

65-66. *Cambodian houses* are usually elevated, to avoid both heat and overflowing canals; above, the view from Phnom Krom, with Tonle Sap in the far distance.

138